PRAYING
is worth
PRAYING

Sayings on Prayer

Larry E. Elliott

BLUEPRINT PRESS
INTERNATIONALE

Scripture quotations marked (NIV) are taken
from the Holy Bible, New International
Version®, NIV®. Copyright © 1973, 1978, 1984,
2011 by Biblica, Inc.™ Used by permission of
Zondervan. All rights reserved worldwide.
www.zondervan.com The "NIV" and "New
International Version" are trademarks
registered in the United States Patent and
Trademark Office by Biblica, Inc.™

ISBN
978-1-961117-13-6 (Paperback)
978-1-961117-14-3 (eBook)
978-1-961117-12-9 (Hardcover)

PRAYING
is worth
PRAYING

Prayer can be the richest, most fulfilling conversation a person can have as he or she talks with the best friend any of us will ever have. This little book is so down to earth, and practical that it is easy every day reading as a reminder of the love God has for us as he communicates with us.

—Dr. Tommy Walter
    Director of Academics and Assistant Professor
    Embry-Riddle Aeronautical University
    Jacksonville, Florida Campus

The disciples asked Jesus, "Teach us to pray" (Luke 11:1). We must learn how to pray. In this book, you will read not only what the Bible says about prayer, but the experiences of those who have sought to understand and practice prayer.

—Dr. Walter Bennett
Retired Director
Education Division
Florida Baptist Convention

Dr. Elliott shows us how to pray out of the core of our lives, which makes it real and exciting. Today, prayer is the most profound need of the church and its members. Prayer is indispensable! Prayer is the most important component of our personal spiritual formation. Having known Larry for thirty-three years, I know he is a praying man. He's not just a theoretician; he's a practitioner. Filled with powerful thoughts and suggestions, this book is simple, but not simplistic. This little tool will help you become a more effective pray-er! I recommend it to the most seasoned Christian scholar or the struggler, who is new to the journey of faith.

—Dr. Ron Rowe
Retired Executive Director
Jacksonville Baptist Association

Acknowledgments

Thanks to my many friends who answered my statement, "Why I believe praying is worth praying." The Lord blesses me with friends, who love the Lord and pray daily. Prayer permeates their lives. When one prays, you feel close to the throne of God. I pray my book will also lead you closer to God.

Dedication

Dedicated to the glory of God, my friend, counselor, confidant, my Lord, and Savior.

Preface

I pray *Praying Is Worth Praying* will increase your prayer life and inspire you to be a prayer partner and a prayer warrior. Read the quotes as you prepare for your daily devotional. The quotes on prayer come from the hearts of those struggling with pain and heartache. The sayings on prayer come from my heart to encourage you to talk more often with God. The quotes from God's Word come from the hearts of those who went before us and experienced prayer's unbelievable power.

My prayer for you: "Lord, bless those who read these words with your presence and power. Fill the words with hope, comfort, and peace. Amen."

Sayings on
Prayer

Looking up to God makes facing the problems of life bearable.

Bowing your head and closing your eyes, closes out the world and lets God in.

Larry E. Elliott

Prayer soothes the heart
and calms the soul.

Make a direct call to God today.
He receives voice mail and the
call is free.

Enjoy a quiet time with God.
He will like it and so will you.

Prayer is an upward look, which
brings a remarkable return.

Larry E. Elliott

Pray as if your life depended on it—and it does!

When you look up, what do you see? A loving God in heaven, who sees you.

Have you prayed today? Pray and enjoy a better day.

Rather than ask God for a blessing, praise Him for His.

A prayer a day keeps
Satan away. If you don't
believe it, try it.

Look to heaven. You may be
surprised by what you see!

Talking to God is like
talking to your best friend.
Talk to Him today and
mention a friend in need.

Do you realize that prayer can
calm the soul, relax the mind,
and give you peace? Try it and
enjoy the results.

Pray and seek God's
will, knowing His will
brings contentment!

Prayer brings blessings from
God to prayer warriors and
prayer partners. Which are you?

Prayer opens a new level of communication with God. The more you pray the closer you get.

Prayer is far better than meditation. Meditation is inward. Prayer is upward.

Pray whether you want to or
not and let God do the rest.

If you want to get close to God,
pray!

Prayer mobilizes Christian faith. Pray and let prayer move you upward today!

When you talk with God, expect results and you will get them!

Larry E. Elliott

Prayer opens doors only God can unlock. Pray today and let God unlock your door!

Have you heard a prayer you like? Did it come from you? Say a prayer today. God will like it.

Why I Believe Praying Is Worth Praying

Praying is the language of God Almighty. Prayer lets Him know we care. Prayer lets Him know we believe. Prayer lets Him know we have faith— faith that He is real, faith that He hears our words, faith enough to know He cares. As the saying: Seeing is not believing, but believing is seeing.

—Jayme

Prayer to me is candidly communicating with Almighty God, the God of the universe. Prayer is what keeps me sane in this insane world.

—Troy

Larry E. Elliott

What comes out of the mouth starts
in the heart. As I pray, I confess the
thoughts of my heart to God and through
this allow God to change and shape
my heart so that I might glorify Him.

—Michael

Prayer is the intimate relationship I have with our Creator and Savior. Prayer is how I confess my love through conversation and repentance. I maintain this daily conversation to continuously strengthen my love for my Father.

—Brady

Jesus Christ defines my definition of prayer. Prayer is a gift, an opportunity to communicate with my Creator, Savior, Sustainer-communicate with a Holy God. He hears, answers, talks with me, and loves me as His disciple.

—SG

Prayer is my "FaceTime" with the Heavenly Father, which is vital in my relationship with Him. My FaceTime connection with Him directs my steps as I walk with Him each day.

—Adam

I stay in contact with my Lord and Savior through daily prayer. I do not like to miss a day without talking to Him. Every time I talk to Him, He gives me strength, through which I can do all things.

—Harold

Prayer is worship and praise for a
loving and beneficent creator. Prayer is
communion with the Redeemer of my soul.

—Kim

Prayer is a personal conversation with God in time of need or praise. I am a better person when God alone is my audience.

—David

GOD'S WORD
SAYS

If my people who are called by my name will humble themselves and pray and seek my face and turn from their wicked ways, them will I hear from heaven and will forgive their sin and will heal their land.

—2 Chronicles 7:14, NIV

O God, you are my God, earnestly
I seek you; my soul thirsts for you,
my body longs for you, in a dry and
weary land where there is no water.

—Psalm 63:1, NIV

Larry E. Elliott

Show me your ways, O Lord, teach me
your paths; guide me in your truth and
teach me, for you are God, my Savior,
and my hope is in You all day long.

—Psalm 25:4-5, NIV

I call on you, O God, for you will answer
me; give ear to me and hear my prayer.
Show me the wonder of your great love,
you who save by your right hand those
who take refuge in you from their foes.
Keep me as the apple of your eye; hide
me in the shadow of your wings from
the wicked who assail me, from my
mortal enemies who surround me.

—Psalm 17:6-9, NIV

Larry E. Elliott

Give ear to my words, O Lord, consider
my sighing. Listen to my cry for help,
my King and my God, for to you I pray.
In the morning, O Lord, you hear my
voice; in the morning I lay my requests
before you and wait in expectation.

—Psalm 5:1-3, NIV

I thank my God every time I remember
you, in all of my prayers for all of you.
I always pray with joy because of your
partnership in the gospel from the first
day until now, being confident that he who
began a good work in you will carry it on to
completion until the day of Christ Jesus.

—Philippians 1:3-5, NIV

Larry E. Elliott

SAYINGS ON PRAYER

Bow your head and close your eyes for a quiet, peaceful time with God.

A prayer in the street is just as good as a prayer in the church. God hears no matter where you are.

Larry E. Elliott

Now I close my eyes to say,
"Thank you, Lord, for another
day." Say a little prayer today
for someone you love.

Prayer lifts us closer to heaven to
hear the still small voice of God.

Prayer relieves stress and brings contentment.

A little prayer is better than no prayer at all. Say a little prayer today.

Larry E. Elliott

In the stillness of a prayer,
you can find peace.

Prayer holds the power to save!
Pray for someone today.

I prayed today and found God eager to hear my prayer. Pray today. He is there for you.

Say a prayer today and calm your soul in the stillness of the moment.

Larry E. Elliott

Enlist a prayer partner to pray
with you and for you. Their
prayer support will bless you
and those for whom you pray.

A prayer for a friend is an
expression of a caring heart.

A little prayer goes a long way.

How do you know God's will?—
Pray and ask Him.

Larry E. Elliott

Pray and experience the unbelievable power of God.

Say a prayer today and listen for the still, small voice of God.

Prayer is a quiet place
to meet God.

Looking up to heaven brings
blessings down to earth.

Larry E. Elliott

Pray with confidence,
God always answers!

Prayer support brings healing
and emotional stability. Pray
daily.

Bless someone you love
today by praying for them.

Pray today as if God is looking
right at you because He is!

Larry E. Elliott

Prayer eases the pain and comforts the heart with peace.

If you ever see prayer at work, you will never cease to pray.

Why I Believe Praying Is Worth Praying

Prayer is an intimate conversation
with God where no one, but
God listens and hears.

—Anonymous

Nothing assures me more than being with my Savior in prayer. I know He is listening to my anxieties, fears, needs, and desires whether in silence or with others. He has a plan for me. Every tear I shed in prayer reminds me of the precious blood He shed for me on Calvary's Cross. Feeling my Savior's overwhelming power and presence provides an unexplainable tranquility knowing my soul is in harmony with Him.

—Ron

Larry E. Elliott

When I have needs, choices, and major decisions, only going to the Lord can help me. Only God knows my heart, life, and future to guide me properly. I cannot explain how an awesome God speaks to me through the Holy Spirit. When He does, I do not question the action I must take. No friend or relative knows what is best for me. Only God. What a friend I have in my time of prayer!

—Pat

Prayer is simply talking with God and telling Him all your troubles. I talked with Him this morning and told Him all my troubles. You will not believe the peace He gave me.

—Larry

Larry E. Elliott

Prayer to me is communing with God;
addressing, listening, hearing, praising,
thanking, honoring, confessing,
and requesting. Prayer is being with
God; magnificent, merciful, gracious,
loving, forgiving, and guiding.

—John

Prayer is communicating with God.
It is glorifying Him, thanking him,
sharing myself with him. It is being
quiet and listening for his guidance.

—Susan

Praying is worth praying because it is our communication with our Lord. As we pray, we ask Him to be our Comforter and guide us through the life we have with Him. He is our provider in good times and bad.

—Charles

Praying gives me the awesome opportunity
to have an intimate conversation
with my Father. A time to express my
gratitude for His unconditional love, to
ask for forgiveness when I disappoint
Him, and to thank Him for all He
has done for me and my family.

—Larry Jr.

Larry E. Elliott

Prayer is the miracle of God by which we share our desires, dreams, and hope. We also share our sorrows, our fears, our sadness while expressing our deep desire for forgiveness of sin.

—Anonymous

GOD'S WORD
SAYS

But you, dear friends, build yourselves up
in your most holy faith and pray in the
Holy Spirit. Keep yourselves in God's love.

—Jude 1:20, NIV

The Lord is far from the wicked, but he hears the prayers of the righteous.

—Proverbs 15:29, NIV

Larry E. Elliott

Never be lacking in zeal, but keep your spiritual fervor, serving the Lord. Be joyful in hope, patient in affliction, faithful in prayer.

—Romans 12:11-12, NIV

Rejoice in the Lord always, I will say
again: Rejoice! Let your gentleness be
evident to all. The Lord is near. Do
not be anxious in anything, but in
everything, by prayer and petition with
thanksgiving, present your requests
to God. And the peace of God, which
transcends all understanding, will guard
your hearts and minds in Christ Jesus.

—Philippians 4:4-7, NIV

Larry E. Elliott

One day, Jesus was praying in a certain place. When he finished, one of his disciples said to him, "Lord, teach us to pray, just as John taught his disciples." Jesus said, "When you pray, say, Our Father who are in heaven."

—Luke 1:1-2, NIV

SAYINGS ON PRAYER

Say a prayer and feel
the presence of God.

Have you thought to pray today?
Think and pray.

Want to know how to
get sunshine in the
midst of rain? Pray.

Spend a quiet moment in
prayer today. Be still and know
I am God.

Larry E. Elliott

Spend a few minutes alone
in prayer with God each day.
You will be surprised the
difference a few minutes make.

If you look for God, He will meet
you face to face.

Prayer expresses a caring
heart for someone loved.

Seek peace and
consolation—Pray.

Larry E. Elliott

A little prayer goes a long way.

When was the last time you had a conversation with God? Have one today. You might be surprised what you hear.

Pray today for someone you love and let God's love flow through you to them.

When was the last time you came face to face with God on your knees? Face God. He will lift you up and place you on solid ground.

Dial God's number, He
will always answer your
call personally.

For a real source of
comfort—Pray

Every prayer you utter graces
the heart of God and fills
your heart with His love.

Prayer uplifts the heart and
replenishes the soul.

Larry E. Elliott

Prayer is not a long distance call, but a short distance from God's heart to yours.

Put your hands together not to clap, but to pray and God will clap with you.

Looking upward in prayer
brings God's love and
compassion down to your heart.

Say a prayer and save a life; the
life you save may be your own.

Larry E. Elliott

Say a little prayer and
make a big difference.

Prayer lifts your spirit and
unites it with the Spirit of God.

Why I Believe Praying Is Worth Praying

Prayer is the most awe-inspiring
and private communication in the
world because it is only known to
God, the keeper of the world's most
abundant and guarded secrets.

—Anonymous

God is the inventor of communication.
While an operator can only plug one wire
into one socket at a time in limited quantity
allowing one person to speak to another,
God plugs billions of lines into His socket
simultaneously hearing and responding to
those calling on Him. No computerized phone
system will ever compare or equal God's.

—Anonymous

Prayer is the one true medium
unaffected by faulty technology
nor miscommunicated by a poor or
biased interpreter, not subject to
rebuttal and is never ignored.

—Anonymous

Prayer is often prejudiced, self-centered, one-sided, and filled with a single agenda. Frequently, we compile our prayers with fear and confusion. Nevertheless, God understands the message and loves the messenger.

—George

Prayer is abundance of feelings, abundance of thoughts, abundance of confusion and, many times, abundance of fear shoved into one cry for help. Only God understands.

—Alfie

Prayer is consistent with the will and design of God's intention in creating mankind to have fellowship with Him. There can be no fellowship with God without communication through prayer.

—Jay

I believe faith and prayer go hand in hand.
One is not effectual without the other.

—JG

Prayer to me is the confession of the heart. When prayer is made at the crossroads of faith, sin is forgiven.

—Anonymous

I believe praying is worth praying
because through prayer despair
transforms into hope.

—Jerri

Sayings on Prayer

Prayer connects us with a
Father who loves us and
willingly takes care of us.

A prayer coupled with love
reaches into the very heart of
God.

Prayer opens the door to heaven
and let's God touch our soul.

When you kneel in prayer, the
Lord kneels with you and never
leaves your side.

Larry E. Elliott

Prayer with God reduces stress
and lowers blood pressure.
Try it and you will see!

As Christians, we are to live our
lives in a spirit of prayer.

Love the Lord with all your
heart and He will never
fail you. He is always ready
to hear your prayer.

Life is worth living when God is
in the midst of it. Prayer puts
you in the midst of it.

Larry E. Elliott

If you have experienced the power of prayer, you know how powerful it is.

A miracle is the greatest result of personal prayer. Try it. You may be surprised with the results!

Sometimes we fail to look up and see God's hand reaching down. Prayer connects us with the hand of God.

Looking for an answer to your problem? Talk to God, He has the answer.

Larry E. Elliott

Prayer is a person's lifeline through which the blessings of God flow!

Look up to heaven, feel God's presence and tell him your troubles. He will respond with love and grace.

Never look down! Always look up! Help is just a prayer away!

What a difference a prayer makes—a difference made in heaven!

Pray expecting a miracle
and you may be surprised!

Prayer is a precious commodity,
which produces amazing
results.

A daily quiet time with
God replenishes the soul
and lifts the spirits.

Prayer is the best medicine for
an upset life.

Larry E. Elliott

Why not pray and let God
have His own way with you?

Have you ever felt the arms of
God around you? Pray and let
God hug you.

Need a friend? Sit down
by yourself and talk to
God. He is the best friend
you will ever have!

Give your burdens to God and
let Him carry them. His arms
will lighten your load.

Larry E. Elliott

Have you ever felt like the words of your prayer never reached beyond the ceiling? When you pray, your words reach the ceiling in heaven.

You are never taller than when you
are on your knees talking to God.

—Unknown

Larry E. Elliott

Have you had a dose of prayer today? Prayer is the medicine which cures spiritual illness.

Why I Believe Praying Is Worth Praying

Nothing is ever lost to God in prayer nor is an absence of prayer a way of hiding things from God. Prayer becomes the sign of understanding between a finite being and an infinite power—God.

—Anonymous

Through prayer, I strengthen my relationship with God. In 1 Thessalonians 5:17, the Bible says, "Pray without ceasing." Repeatedly, I have seen God's faithfulness through the fervent prayer of His people.

—Mary

Larry E. Elliott

Why do I believe in the power of prayer? Because I've seen it, felt it in my life, and most of all, need the power of prayer each day. I am grateful God is with me always.

—Becky

Prayer gets me through the hard times and makes the good times sweeter. I know God has a plan for me, which I might not see unless I talk to Him through prayer.

—Heidi

Larry E. Elliott

Prayer works because God is good!
Think of it! You can childishly ask the
"Creator of the Universe" for anything,
and He loves you enough to give you
what is absolutely best for you!

—Karen

I believe in the power of prayer because it brings me through difficult times. I praise God when He answers my prayers. Prayer is just between me and God and I can talk to Him anytime and anywhere. God knows my needs and He wants me to talk to Him about them. I thank God I am His child and when I confess my sins to Him in prayer, He forgives me.

—Amanda

Larry E. Elliott

Talking with God gives me inner peace. Life can be hard, but I always know God is in charge. Therefore, I can talk to Him anytime of the day, asking, thanking, praising, seeking guidance from Him no matter how hard the times become.

—Vicki

The best day of my life was when I prayed
to Jesus to come into my heart and
wash all my sins away and He did! God
may not answer my prayers on my time
schedule or give the answer I want to
hear, but He will always answer them.

—Reen'e

Prayer to me means more than just asking for things. Prayer means praising, worshipping, and seeking forgiveness. I usually spend more time asking than anything else. I feel closer to God when I pray and can't believe He actually wants to hear from me. Whether God answers my prayers the way I want or not, I know He listens to me and gives me the peace only He can give.

—Joy

WHAT I BELIEVE ABOUT PRAYER...

Why I believe praying
is worth praying...

How God answered my prayer(s)...

My favorite prayer...

Today I will pray for...

Prayer Builds Better Lives
Through Better Living

In his first book *Experiencing the Miracle Power of God,* Doctor Elliott writes about the many miracles God performed in his life from his salvation experience through college and his ministry through the Florida Baptist Convention. Available now online and in local bookstores in hardback, paperback and ebook.

About the Author

Born in Hapeville, Georgia, Doctor Elliott accepted the Lord at the age of twelve and surrendered to the full-time gospel ministry one week later. As a pastor, he served churches in Texas and Florida for over ten years. As a member of the Florida Baptist Convention staff, he served Florida Baptist churches for twenty-seven years. He holds the unique distinction of Chaplain Emeritus of the Florida Air National Guard. Presently, he and his wife reside in Jacksonville. He teaches a senior adult Bible study, plays in the church orchestra, and enjoys writing.